CONVERSATIONS WITH WELL SEASONED WOMEN

CONVERSATIONS WITH WELL SEASONED WOMEN:

EXPLORE THE BEAUTY AND WISDOM OF AGE

Jan M. Whalen, MASL
Whalen Voices Publishing

Phoenix, AZ

Conversations with Well Seasoned Women:
Explore the Beauty and Wisdom of Age

Jan M. Whalen, MASL

Copyright ©2022 by Jan M. Whalen, MASL
Published by Whalen Voices Publishing
Phoenix, Arizona
623 466-5067
jan@whalenvoices.com
www.whalenvoices.com

ISBN: 978-09705714-1-0
Cover Design: Diego Paredes Instagram: @una.bestia
Page Design: Jan M. Whalen and Carol Waltz of
Bella Media Management

Printed in the United States of America.

To my wise husband Ross McCollum, who
sees the beauty of my seasoned age.

CONTENTS

INTRODUCTION

Life is beautiful, and if we are lucky enough to be alive, we owe it to ourselves to celebrate. With each passing decade, we've beaten the odds once more. So as a fellow survivor of life, I'd like to invite you to call yourself *Well Seasoned* instead of "old."

Even though it's very common, the word old is actually the wrong word to describe your age. The dictionary says old means: no longer in use, obsolete, discarded, discredited, and outmoded. While old might describe a car or a washing machine, it's not the best way to describe a person's age.

Discussing advanced age is usually not flattering. When I was 35 (yes, the ripe "old" age of 35!), I competed in Taekwondo tournaments in a division called Senior Women. I remember how insulting that was. In other settings folks awkwardly trip over words like mature, elderly, senior, geriatric, and my favorite—a woman of a certain age.

When the Persian poet Rumi spoke about different ages, he had three categories: uncooked, cooked and burning. It's been my experience that the very young (uncooked) have not had enough experiences to be as interesting as they will be when they are cooked by life, and even better, when they've lived long enough to transfer wisdom to younger generations (burning with information). Burning reminds me of a flaming marshmallow blackened to perfection over a campfire, but that's just me.

Who am I to correct Rumi? Yet, I prefer to use the

word Seasoned because it implies zest, sizzling with spicy wisdom. Wisdom is like fine wine; it's the accumulation of processing experiences over a lifetime. My intention is for you to explore your own wisdom when you hear the stories of others.

The word Beauty, part of this book's subtitle, doesn't seem to fit with conversations of Age, yet Beauty is a perfect companion to wisdom. Consider beauty in four categories: visual attractiveness, great courage, unassuming generosity, and delightful surprises. As a Well Seasoned person, life has certainly surprised you with great beauty, courage and generosity. This book is a collection of short reflections, making it a quick read. The categories are: Age, Worth, Confidence, Friends, Writing and an Invitation.

Age: How can a young person know time and age? You'll be filled with joy to read about 102 years vibrant Anna Marie Peterson, the most well seasoned woman I have ever known. A true role model, she lived until almost 105 and kept her mind and body active each day, showing us that we don't need to blame age for every ill.

Worthy: Life is art. Living would be a whole lot easier if we felt our own beauty and value. You'll read about ways to train your mind and see yourself and your voice in artistic terms. When you feel worthy, you eliminate the blocks that keep you from reaching your purpose.

Confidence: Everyone benefits from feeling more confident. In this section, you'll experience tricks of the trade from my former voice coach Dr. Ralph Hillman. Adjusting your attitude, keeping promises and knowing yourself will also boost your confidence.

Friends: A life without friends is not worth living. This section is filled with the ins and outs of friendship, and also invaluable advice from a couple of my Well Seasoned friends to help you live a happier and more productive life.

Writing: You'll be surprised about what you can learn about yourself through writing. No matter what your spiritual beliefs, inspiration is all around—even when you recall your favorite shoe stories. My goal is to motivate you to write.

The last section of the book is an **Invitation**, and its purpose is to give ideas on how you can connect with Whalen Voices to take advantage of what we offer. If you have enjoyed this book, you might be willing to share a story or give a response to something you've read. Even if you disagree, we'd love to hear your perspective. When women discuss, things get interesting. We want you to become a part of our Whalen Voices community.

My hope is that this book gives you something to think about and much to write about. Take it from someone who had never considered herself a writer (me), it's great fun to explore, record and express your human experiences through writing. Enjoy.

Conversations

The original book, *Well Seasoned: The Beauty of Age* was filled with these same 22 essays. *Conversations with Well Seasoned Women* also includes a set of questions at the end of each section: A leader/study guide.

The beauty of this guide comes from the host of women (and a few good men) who sat down with me to create the questions.

I asked each person to imagine leading a group in a

discussion of one of the 22 essays. As a former teacher, I could have created questions myself, yet it's also true that when two or more get together, the results are nothing short of magic!

While we were working together on #15, Julie made an astute observation: "All of what I've just said is my opinion, and it comes from my experiences." She opened me up to a new thought: our deepest convictions, our best questions and our most interesting observations arise out of our personal experiences.

Reflecting upon our experiences with a group of individuals is one of the most powerful teachers on the planet. Our lives are colored by our unique history with: parents, jobs, educations, homes, bosses, and friends. These factors spice up our lives and allow us to interpret our journey from different vantage points.

Whether you are reading this book solo or with a group, grab a journal to record your reflections, thoughts, inspirations, and wisdom regarding the topics.

Leadership Tip for Group Discussions: The "Yes And" Game

This game originated in the world of improv, and has been borrowed time and again as a great way to generate ideas while honoring what everyone says. The game is simple. When someone makes a suggestion, the next speaker (and all others who follow) honors what was just said with the words, "Yes, and..." then offers their thoughts, comments, inspirations or ideas.

Can you see the beauty of this game? First of all, everyone feels freer to share because they know that rather than being cut down or thrown under the bus, their ideas will find acceptance. The next person will offer their own suggestions with the same assurance. Before you know it, a plethora of possibilities (wisdom) emerges. Brain-storming at its best!

As a leader, you will undoubtedly give your own thoughts about the questions, yet this game encourages everyone's engagement. Enjoy your conversations, filled with the diversity of perspectives of everyone present.

AGE

"Taking a holistic approach to life has made this transition into a new decade much easier. It has been a time of reflection. It has been a journey of self-actualization.

~Linda Garza Kalaf, 60
from *You are the Perfect Age*

Seasoned Age

You walk through age
in resilient shoes that
support your confidence
and guide your direction.

Seasoned age is a time to
gather the soul-friends who
stood by you in every season.

You know your value because
you see challenges from both sides.
Celebrate the gift of wisdom,
this path of your humanity.

The art of creating a life
with courage and forgiveness
is your greatest achievement.
May your heart be set on fire
with the voice of gratitude.

1.

NOT WHAT I EXPECTED

If I had a quarter for every time I heard someone say, "I never expected my life would be like this," I'd be so rich, I could take all of my readers on a cruise around the world. I have to admit that I've said those words myself, yet why are we surprised by life? When we first dream about the future, we are new at being human. We don't have the capacity to see the vastness of the world, the nasty snares and ten-thousand pitfalls along the way—or the joys and the beautiful moments. We don't know what we don't know.

Recently, two 20-ish women admitted to me that they don't feel as confident in themselves now as compared to when they were in high school. I suspect that in high school, unencumbered by fear, their confidence came from a place of naiveté. I love the boldness of youth, yet the vision of youth has blinders. We are most curious and least cautious during this season.

Many of us leave home around 18 to enjoy the freedom of the world. It might be an unpleasant surprise to discover that there aren't as many supportive people to catch, comfort and pick us up when we fall. When life comes at us, it doesn't take many battles to realize that the world can be a cold place. As a result, self-doubt creeps in.

Everyone faces challenges. Stuff happens to all of us. Unplanned events present themselves from time to time:

accidents, floods, untimely deaths, operations, lost jobs, lost homes, families, and last and certainly not most critical, (but can really be the straw that breaks the camel's back), our favorite TV show gets canceled.

Whenever I get in a funk about all this, I look to my wise friends for inspiration. Even in bad times, one friend says, "I'm so blessed," while another tells me, "I take it one day at a time," or, "This tragedy brought our family together."

Knowing that my brother John is not likely to walk on his own again doesn't keep him from adapting so that he can drive and hunt. He lives his life by counting what he can do—and his wife faces her own adjustments with grace. Courageous people inspire me.

Dad used to say, "Play the hand you were dealt." He said it so often, we had it engraved on his headstone. My interpretation of his words is that no matter what unpleasant things comes into our lives, we are better off accepting what we can't change and resourcefully making the best life possible.

We have a choice. If life has surprised us in negative ways, we can either resent each day we have, or transform our lives into something unique, meaningful and sizzling.

Go for the sizzle.

Your Conversation Questions

Ruth Vaske is a wife, mother of six children, two grandchildren, and enjoys her career as a flight attendant. She has met people from all corners of the earth during her life's journey. She's known for her curiosity, compassion, encouragement and thoughtfulness. These are the questions she'd like to ask you:

1. What expectations did you have for your life when you were: a child, a teen, in your 20s, now.

2. We all have faced the "pitfalls" of life. How did your life change when you faced some of your challenges? Ruth's examples are: not getting into a college, a lost love, an accident.

3. We feel more "free" in high school than other times in our lives. Explain why you either agree or disagree with this statement.

4. Has there been a time in your life when you have not felt supported, so you had to find strength from within yourself? Explain.

5. Who has inspired you? Whose voice do you hear inside your head when you need help, encouragement or direction?

6. How would you describe the "hand you were dealt"? What opportunities came from your "hand"?

7. Do you keep a favorite quote in your home or office to encourage you? If so, what is it?

2.

WELL SEASONED WOMAN: ANNA MARIE

PETERSON

You know you've arrived when your name is announced to a crowd, followed by your age, followed by wild applause. Welcome to the world of Anna Marie Peterson, born on December 5, 1916. Having celebrated 104 birthdays, and passing before she reached 105, she remains the most well seasoned woman I've ever known! Recently, she was an active member of P.E.O. (Philanthropic Educational Organization), a studio art group, an exercise group, and Willowbrook Methodist church. She owned her own home, and could be seen at a variety of events with her daughter, Betty Hahn.

This interview with Anna Marie took place when she was 102. She smiled when I ask if she used email. "Well of course, and I have a Facebook account and when I was 97, I started a blog. I show pictures of wall hangings that I make, and write comments about family or I write some saying. I've met interesting people online. I do it by myself and have been using the computer for 15 years or more."

Imagine Anna Marie as a girl about a hundred years ago (way before computers) playing on the tire swing or in the hay mow; see her picking wild flowers along the side of the road and then bringing the cows back from the field at super time. She admits, "When I was a girl, what we did for excitement was not very exciting." She remembers visiting cousins, peeling potatoes forever for the thrashers at noon, riding in the Model T Ford, and using the outhouse complete with a Sears catalog. "It was not pleasant," she remembers, "but we managed."

As a young girl, she was always a church-goer. "I always memorized whole chapters of the Bible and I wanted to be a missionary like my relatives who went to China, Africa and Guatemala. I thought that would be great, but when I grew up, I decided that was not the thing to do."

Anna Marie graduated from Iowa State College with a major in Home Economic Applied Arts two weeks before she got married. She remembers her husband telling her, "'It doesn't matter what grades you get because you'll get the same job anyway—my wife.'" She added, "I didn't realize I was actually using my education by the choices I made in what the kids wore, and furnishings for the house." Little did she know she would eventually have three children, seven grandchildren, 23 great grandchildren and two great-great grandchildren.

After reading *Powers of Two: Finding the Essence of Innovation in Creative Pairs* by Joshua Wolf Shenk, I've wondered if an important aspect of Anna Marie's life has been her long-term partnerships.

She was married for 73 years, spending the early years dedicated to her family. She began playing organ in church as a teenager, and by the time she retired at age 86, she provided music for three services each Sunday. In addition, she played for all the weddings, funerals and choir practices—for a total of 70 years, with 57 years in one church.

After her children were grown, she and her husband collected stamps and worked with stamp dealers into their 90s. "I did Excel spreadsheets for my husband's stamp collection on the computer. He had an enormous collection that took hundreds of pages to record." She also collected Scandinavian stamps. "I started with the first Norwegian stamps and I worked hard to collect stamps and it was very complete up to about 1990."

She partnered with her father on a project that enhanced the quality of her life and perhaps the longevity of his as well. "I can tell you about a time when I helped my father who was 97. After his heart attack, he came to live with us and he needed something to do. He had been a shoemaker all his life, so I started him making wall hangings. I drew patterns on latch hook canvas and he used a punch hook making them into lovely wall hangings. He enjoyed creating things for others to enjoy and made a total of 276 wall hangings. I think he lived longer because he felt useful and it kept me busy drawing them."

Anna Marie made 50 quilts and many smaller wall hangings even before she moved to Sun City. Eleven years ago, she joined a Studio Art Group and entered an art show at the West Valley Art Museum with her daughter Betty, an accomplished artist.

At the age of 91, she was accepted into her first show. Betty taught her how to create needle-felted wall hangings [piercing tufts of raw wool using a very sharp needle with tiny barbs to sculpt various shapes and figures]. Anna Marie loved it, and used flowers, birds, animals and landscapes as her subjects. That's when she wrote to members of the Professional Nature Photographers of India to see if she could use their photographs as the inspiration for her wall hangings. "I'd say, 'I really like your photo. May I use your photograph as inspiration for my work?' They all said yes, and began to call me Granny or that 'little old lady in America.' Then they invited me to become a member of their group."

Enjoying a long life seems to be a family norm for Anna Marie. Her father lived to be 106, her mom's sister, 103, and numerous other relatives on both sides of the family lived well into their 90s.

I was curious about how Anna Marie would answer the same four questions I asked other women in *You are the Perfect Age*. Here is what she said:

What have you learned so far in your life?

~If you have a positive attitude it helps your health and life runs smoothly along. My back hurts every day, but I just get up and ignore it. It's really mind over matter. I tell myself that if I'm not feeling good, tomorrow will be better.

~Curiosity and friends enrich your days. I have gotten so old that everybody else has passed away—all my old friends are gone. But I have quilting friends, art friends, and P.E.O. friends. I think I have more friends now than I did when I was home in Des Moines, Iowa.

~Courage to try new experiences leads to success and happiness.

How do you celebrate your birthday?

I've celebrated more in last 10 years than ever before. When I was a girl we had the family there with birthday cake and that was it.

I was happy to reach 100 and looked forward to more exciting years. I was honored with celebrations for my 99th, 100th and 102nd birthdays by Arts HQ Gallery. Some of my art was shown and, of course, beautiful cakes were enjoyed by many friends.

What goals do you have for the future?

More art pieces will be made and hopefully accepted in juried shows. I have been fortunate in having 100% participation so far in local galleries. My lovely daughter assists me in all my fun experiences and my son does all my framing. I am blessed!

I want to keep up with exercise twice a week and attend church each week.

What makes you worry?

What could I have to worry about? Nothing.

In years past, I suppose I had things I stewed about when my kids were growing up. Betty was the first born and we have never had an argument.

I tell people to be happy all the time, and not worry about things. It's a choice. I look in the mirror and smile at myself and tell myself to have a happy day. We are in a longevity study at Boswell hospital. The survey asks about how I face changes in my life. I just stay happy and don't think bad thoughts. Always. It's attitudinal.

So who is the old person in the room? Certainly not 104 year old Anna Marie Peterson. Living is art, and perhaps when we feel upset or worried about what age will bring, we will envision Anna Marie's smile and gentle reminder that with each new day, we get to make more art—because each life is truly a work of art.

NOTE: As mentioned, Anna Marie Peterson (as we say in P.E.O.), entered Chapter Eternal just a few months before celebrating 105 years of living. She instructed her family to celebrate her life with a party. And they did.

Your Conversation Questions:

Patricia Tomlin has selected these questions to discuss. Patricia is a former teacher, leader and has been president of Chapter DH of P.E.O, during the Covid years. She's the person you'd want to lead meetings, make decisions with assurance, and bring a sense of direction to any group. Here are her questions:

1. Anna Marie's husband commented that her grades would not determine her job because she would get the job of being his wife. This seems to be something that women would not want to hear today. When you graduated from high school or college, what were your expectations for yourself?

2. Other than using the outhouse and bringing in the cows, were some of Anna Marie's activities as a young girl in any way similar to some of your own childhood activities?

3. How have your long-term relationships affected your life and growth as a person? What are some of the best relationships in your life?

4. Have you partnered with your parent on a project? Do you have a parent (or friend) who is aging and for whom you could provide some distraction from their aging process? Explain.

5. Anna Marie said, "What do I have to worry about?" How is your "worry meter" and what do you do to prevent yourself from worrying?

6. Anna Marie is incredibly positive about her future. It is a choice.   How are you choosing to look at your future?

WORTHY

"Worthy Now. Not if. Not when. We are all worthy of love and belonging now. Right this minute. As is."

~Brené Brown

3.

THE RIGHT SHOES

Most women have a sizzling love affair with shoes. We love them for how they look, how they make *us* look and for how they make us feel. As age and reflection bring wisdom to our doors, so has our shoe-attitude changed. After speaking with seasoned women about shoes, it seems safe to say that we care less about what others think and more about how they partner with us to take us where we want to go—a friend and a protector of sorts—to ground and keep us safe. We're no longer a slave to all the latest trends—if they don't fit our lifestyle, budget and taste, we're not interested.

Resilient shoes protect us from harm when we climb on rocks. Cherry red slides bring a pop of color to a basic black outfit, reminding us that we are unique individuals. During seminars, my favorite question is: What is your shoe story? EVERYONE has a shoe story or two. Here's my favorite, taken from my book *Rock Solid Confidence: Presenting Yourself with Assurance, Poise and Power:*

> I'd been looking for that trendy shoe; a cross between sandal and boot. I found a wonderful pair, but the heels were stilettos—much taller than my usual. The salesperson,

Tom, persuaded me to try them on anyway. So I did. Despite the fact that I felt like I was standing on my tippy toes, this new height gave me the ability to look straight into Tom's eyes. I realized I was instantly, lushly tall. He saw the gleam in my eyes and suggested that I "walk in them for a while." So I did, and I fell in love with my new height, despite the fact that my right foot was beginning to hurt.

After much self-debate, I decided to get them. After all, they were on sale and (compelling reason #2), if I didn't like them, I could give them to my niece, Monica, who wears the same size. Never mind she's already 5'11" and why would she want my leftover shoes? I made my decision and when I took them off I barely noticed that my left ankle was sore, and I had to take twelve steps or so before the kinks in each step disappeared. So I got the magic shoes and kept them until the spell broke—thirty minutes later. My better judgment told me to take them back before I hurt myself. What was I thinking?

I'll tell you what I was thinking. I was thinking that it would be nice to have long legs to match my long feet. I was thinking that I could instantly seem thinner and maybe even younger. There was a lot of thinking going on.

Mrs. Eugene McCarthy, politician's wife, once said, "I am who I am. I look the way I look and I am my age." To that, I must add, "And I am just as tall as I am, so get over it!" This is an example where the wish to be more, the fear of not being enough, and the hope of being perfect overshadowed the mastery of self-acceptance.

We love our shoes. Like a collector of anything else (guns, coins, key chains), we love to get them and bring them home. Maybe we store them in the closet just to own them, or save them for a time when they'll come in handy. After all, they take us where we want to go, and offer foundational support along the way.

Where will your shoes take you today?

Your Conversation Questions:

Amber Roelofs multitasks her work while being a wife and raising three small children with humor and grace. A lawyer by profession (passing the bar while pregnant), her eyes sparkle with personality and she's whip smart. Amber suggests these discussion questions:

1. How do you feel about shoes? Do you love them, tolerate them, or something in between?

2. Has your attitude or expectations changed towards the shoes you purchase as you've gotten older? What is the same and what is different?

3. How do the shoes in your closet compare to those that were there a decade ago?

4. How do your shoes reflect what's going on in your life?

5. What are three or four factors you consider before purchasing a pair of shoes?

6. Is there a connection between your shoe choices and your self-esteem and confidence level?

4.

HAIRSPRAY FOR THE MIND

Maybe it's just me, but I am told by a number of advisors to focus, focus, focus my thoughts. Sometimes I wish I had a spray that kept my mind from wandering, the way hairspray keeps my locks from blowing in the wind.

On the other hand, I wonder if there is value in not being focused. I know, it seems almost sacrilegious to make this suggestion in a world filled with goals, but what about a little day dreaming before we set sail? What about letting our minds wander into the land of collective creativity? I'm pretty sure there is such a place.

Let me suggest three ways to let your mind ebb and flow creatively:

Dream naps are fun, not only because you have an excuse to sleep, but also because they're filled with great information. A few years ago, while preparing for a presentation on the topic of confidence for the Arizona Authors Association, I was having trouble choosing a title for my talk. Before the nap I asked myself which title would engage the audience. Mysteriously, when I woke up, the words "Rock Solid Confidence" came to mind. I liked it so much, I used it for the title of my first book.

Meditation followed by writing is an effective way to

discover what your conscious mind doesn't know. Meditation is thinking about nothing, in other words, dreaming up something by NOT thinking about it—a counterintuitive "activity." Try it, it works. There are several ways to meditate, but many find success by sitting in a comfortable position, while focusing on a lit candle. To engage other senses, add incense and music. This solo activity frees the mind from thinking about doing the laundry or scrubbing the floor. Then, grab a journal and write. It takes a bit of self-trust to pick up a pen after being quiet for awhile, yet some thought usually arrives. Be grateful, rather than judgmental, about what you write.

Water is relaxing, whether you are walking near the ocean or taking a shower. In fact, Wallace J. Nichols wrote *Blue Mind: Mental Health Benefits of Being Near Water*, based on scientific research of the health benefits of water. Just going to the ocean or walking near a lake increases the feel-good hormones of dopamine, serotonin and oxytocin; and reduces stress level hormones like cortisol. I love it when science proves what we all know to be true.

As you consider your next big thing to decide, get a little wild in your head. By using some of these methods of releasing the old and welcoming the new, you'll be set to move forward with confidence. And then once you get to a point of decision, focus on your goal as if you were applying a professional-strength-extra-hold hair spray to your mind.

Your Conversation questions:
Linda Garza Kalaf is fond of saying "Yes you can!" and believes it with all her heart. Family means the world to Linda. Her life's work and passion have been in human

resources, diversity and inclusion; with an extensive career in the transportation industry, both air and ground. Most recently, she can be found teaching yoga, with the goal of assisting individuals on their journey of transformation. She has seven suggested questions for you:

1. Are you a person who finds it easy to focus on what you are doing or are you easily distracted? Explain.

2. When you daydream, what does that look like for you?

3. How can daydreaming assist you in setting your goals?

4. We are the creators of our world. Where is your favorite place to go (physically or in your imagination) that gives you a calm, peaceful and safe feeling?

5. Meditation is described as a state of freeing your mind. It's also described as listening to God. What benefits come with meditation?

6. Scientific research reports that when we are near water, creativity is enhanced. Have you found this to be true? Explain.

7. What is the relationship between living authentically and being true to your values?

5.

THE ART OF YOU: A MASTERPIECE

Each day invites us to celebrate the fact that we are rare and wonderful works of art, created by The Master. Not only have we been created with care, we've been given freedom to design a life for ourselves—the "work of art" becomes the artist.

The Elements of Art will be our guide. You may remember studying these building blocks of design in school: Line, Shape, Form, Space, Texture, Color, and Value. So if we are artists, how do these elements of art translate to designing a life?

Let's take a look:

LINE is longer than it is wide, and can be straight or curved. Our journey through life mirrors the line. Life takes many twists and turns, zigs and zags. Life seems to go on forever, but we know that we are merely line segments, having a beginning and an end. Some paths lead to predictable outcomes (consequences). Even though we hope to spare our children, friends, and family pain, their course may provide the necessary lessons they need to learn; sometimes we do more damage giving unsolicited advice. After all, it's their line segment, their life.

SHAPE is a closed line. The Ancient Celtic people loved circles. Square shapes seem strong, while triangles lead our eyes upward. Bodies are described as shapes: pear, oval, flat, angular. Our bodies are like physical homes that make it possible to be an individual living on Earth. Sometimes I envy tall shapes, and yet my height (unless I'm wearing heels) is pretty well set. Physical shape is part hereditary and part reflection of the choices we make. The good news is, if we don't like our shape—we are works in progress—change is possible! Serenity comes in knowing which things we can change and which things we need to accept.

FORM is a three-dimensional shape. That certainly fits us! Not only do we have length and width, but depth as well. Well Seasoned Age brings the possibility of becoming more interesting, more multi-dimensional. We have the opportunity to grow through reflecting on the role-models we imitate, on heartaches we survived, and a thousand life lessons.

SPACE is the area between and around objects. We need space in myriad ways. Just as poetry is a blend of words and silence, we need a balance of rest and activity, of being alone and being with people, of nature and civilization, of being quiet and speaking out. It's even healthy for a couple to spend time apart, creating space for their individuality. Reflection is the silence we need to understand the noise of our lives. A wonderful formula given to us by Carl Koch, head of our Master of Arts in Servant Leadership program is: Experience + Reflection = Wisdom. Carl reminds us that if we don't take time to reflect upon our experiences, we become old people with no wisdom.

TEXTURE can be seen and felt. It might be rough or smooth, hard or soft. As humans, I imagine texture as the grit we gain from overcoming obstacles. Our "bad" habits or challenging events can destroy us—as a fire destroys or refine us. Our quirky aspects may be considered flaws by some, yet that's what makes us real and lovable. Accepting our contradictions as the texture of our essence makes for an artistic life.

COLOR expresses emotion, mood, and brings life to the visual artist's story. The condition of our health can be detected by tones in skin—looking pale, or washed out, for example. We color our hair, strategically wear colored clothing to enhance our eyes and skin; even our voices have color. (See the next story.) The art of life is to love and accept the colors we can not change and change the ones we can.

VALUE refers to the lightness or darkness of a color. We use the word value when it comes to grayscale photographs, as they are actually many shades of gray. (I'm not sure if there are 50 or not.) Some people seem shiny, like glitter, while others appear to be hiding their true essence under a dusty blanket. When I met LaRae years ago, the first thing I noticed was her radiant smile. Immediately, I wanted to be her friend. The best part of meeting someone face to face is to experience the essence that surrounds them—looking into one's eyes, we witness their hidden beauty first hand.

As in the saying, "We're in this alone together," we are ultimately responsible for the elements we blend into our lives. We have the opportunity and the responsibility to uplift, encourage and cheer each other forward.

We all win when we perceive each person's journey as a rare and priceless work of art.

Your Conversation Questions:

Jamise Liddell, Ph.D. is an educational consultant and training designer—an Instructional Systems Specialist (ISS). This woman is a powerhouse of knowledge and exudes wisdom. Here are her suggested conversation questions:

1. Who do you consider to be an artist? Might we all be artists in some way?

2. Which words or phrases have the word "line" in them? For example: lifeline, timeline, walk the line.

3. Does the power of physical shape intertwine with attraction?

4. What "textures" of people do you encounter in your daily life. Examples: Rough, Teflon.

5. What role does color play in your life? Possible examples: Skin color, hair color, clothing colors.

6. What we believe about ourselves is the value we place upon it. How do you calculate value? Money? Beauty? Other?

7. Would you ever have thought that the Elements of Art fit your life? Does it make sense to you? Explain.

6.

WHAT COLOR IS YOUR VOICE?

Have you ever thought about the color of your voice? Some of us apply color to our faces and hair to enhance our natural beauty, but what about the color radiating from your inner world through the words you speak and tones you habitually choose?

Let's have some fun with the idea of color in your voice. No particular color is good or bad, but blending the right color combinations will help you reach your communication goals.

A **Light Gray** voice has a matter-of-fact, unemotional color, with little inflection and continuous sound, a stereotypical engineer tone. This color serves us well when we want to appear calm, and is standard in business situations.

The second, **Dark Gray**, emits a grave tone. Listen to the words that go with this color and you'll hear sarcasm and negativity. While it's useful to be realistic, be careful not to make this the only color you speak.

Big Bold Red is the next category. We tend to be a bit intimidated by this high-intensity voice. Its boldness dominates so much, there's no room for opposing opinions. Think Meryl Streep in *The Devil Wears Prada* dismissing her employees with, "That's All." Red words are staccato, short and detached. Some see this as a leadership or coach's tone.

Metallic Pink My favorite voice is this energetically flashy Metallic Pink. A high intensity voice (like Red), it boldly dances with enthusiasm and jazz. It's the most interesting, for short periods of time, but like salt, a little goes a long way. While the Gray voice might seem dull, it does feel credible. The Metallic Pink voice can be entertaining, but might not be taken seriously. A perfect blend of Gray and Pink will bring both excitement and credibility.

Denim Blue Think light denim, like your favorite pair of jeans or the color of the sky on a sunny day. This voice is welcoming, friendly and cheerful. It has the flow used by steady leaders because of its authenticity. Of course, taken to extremes, this "nice" voice may be seen as too pastel to lead. When the Denim Blue asks questions for clarity, it may be misinterpreted as weakness by Red voices. Adding a little Red is sometimes helpful—and Red mixed with Blue is Purple, the royal color!

Over the years, in working with clients of all ages, I've noticed that voices vary in tone and intensity. You might ask,"What difference does it make?" According to my first voice coach, Dr. Ralph Hillman, when we speak, not only do others hear us, but more importantly, we hear and feel the tone, or color, we use 24/7. This affects our attitude, self-esteem and mood.

No voice is one color, and various situations call for modifications, which is easier to do than to change your clothes! If you're having difficulty deciding which color you use most often, ask a trusted friend this question: "If my voice were a color, which color would it be?"

Which colors do you aspire to speak?

Your Conversation Questions:

I've called upon my three brothers to lend their own Whalen Voices to this book. All fine men! Len is a Chiropractor in Florida; Ralph, a retired guidance counselor who worked in Taipei, Taiwan now living in Florida; John owns his own farm in Minnesota with his wife, Ellen. They want to know:

1. Are you happy with the color of the voice you usually use? Explain.

2. When you've never met someone in person, but you speak with them by phone, how does their voice affect your perception of how they look or the type of person they are? Given an example.

3. Which situations in your current life call for a Light Gray voice?

4. When would a Bold Red voice be effective for you to use?

5. Only five voice colors were named. Can you think of others? Describe them.

6. How does the color of one's voice change with their daily roles? For example: teacher, coach, leader, counselor, parent, doctor.

7. How might thinking about your voice's color help you in relationships? How does your voice color change when you are dating? When you're in the middle of a disagreement?

7.

THE SOUL FELT ITS WORTH

When anyone asks me to name my favorite Christmas carol, I choose "Oh Holy Night." The truth is, the six words I love are: "…and the soul felt its worth." Unlike most significant lyrics, it's only sung once in the beginning, so you have to be ready to hear it.

To me, those who feel worthy have a great advantage in life. Self-worth carries the key to our self-esteem and confidence. Without it, low expectations and apathy grip us. My dad used to say, "I feel like a penny waiting for change." It was a clear indication that he didn't feel very worthy and he transferred that perspective to his children. He also used to wonder out loud if Len and I, the oldest of his eight children, were "college material."

We all have our talents and skills, faults and shortcomings. Not everyone can run a marathon, paint a masterpiece or act in a play; yet all people have worth. It's sad to know that we hold ourselves back from what we want to do, apologize for mistakes we make, and sabotage our good intentions—all based on the lie of low self-worth.

In 2017, we watched "CNN Heroes: Everyday People Changing the World" award show. Actress Diane Lane introduced Amy Wright, who started a coffee shop, Bitty &

Beau's (https://www.bittyandbeauscoffee.com). This unique coffee shop builds the self-worth of its 40 employees with intellectual and developmental disabilities. They've just opened another location and plan to add 20 more!

As a mom of four children—two with disabilities— Amy's story is compelling. When she learned that many young people with disabilities never work, she thought *No*. That was the moment she envisioned a coffee shop to change the trajectory for this demographic. My soul jumped through the air during her acceptance speech when she said these words: "Bitty and Beau, I know you are watching and I want you to know that I wouldn't change you for the world, but I will change the world for you."

If, for some reason, you don't have an "Amy" to change the world for you, don't "…lay in sin and error pining…." Know that you have a purpose and a mission to make a difference. Find it. Follow it.

Maybe that's why I'm passionate about storytelling in general (and my classes specifically). One very good way to build your self-worth is by remembering your successes, telling the story of how you have overcome obstacles, and how you, in many small ways, have changed the world for yourself and others.

Dr. Len Whalen will tell you that you are worthy.

Your Conversation Questions:

Sharon Foster, Ph.D. has devoted much of her life to education as a teacher and school administrator. Her creative spirit has taken her into other industries with a sense of adventure. Sharon brings wisdom and grace to everyone fortunate enough to know her. Here are Sharon's suggested discussion questions:

1. What constitutes worth or value? Can it be described as: words, concepts, feelings, a sense?

2. Name five kinds of worth. Example: financial worth

3. How do you know you feel worthy?

4. What is self-worth and soul-worth? Are they different or interconnected?

5. Where does worth come from? Is it something you are born with? Inherited? Earned? Is it a part of your personality?

6. Would you be willing to share a story that is an example of soul-worth or self-worth? The story can be from your life or someone you know.

CONFIDENCE

"Confidence is the self-assurance and boldness we posses to make decisions, take risks, ask for what we want, feel sure of what we're doing and live with zest."

~Jan Whalen, *Rock Solid Confidence*

8.

RESOURCEFUL: A MAGIC WORD

Rock-solid confidence has nothing to do with what others think of us. It comes from the trust we have in ourselves to decide what we want, and to step-up to our goals.

The other day I was telling a friend about my challenging day (imagine an annoying whine), not knowing what to do next. Without batting an eyelash, she said, "But you're resourceful, so you'll figure it out."

Maybe it was true. I remembered a time when I planned a painting day with my sixth grade social studies classes, with 120 kids in six, forty-minute periods. I had no idea how I was going to accomplish the task, but I took a chance, worked out a system, and made time for clean-up. At the end of the paint day (with only two major spills), the mission was accomplished.

Yes, resourceful am I—and so are you. My friend offers us a rare gift by helping us remember that we are like the leading lady in a movie—we have the power to slay the dragon, win the race and quiet the wild animals. Based on our successes of the past, including small victories like painting days, we can manage the future.

What does it mean to be resourceful? How does it show up in your life? Resourceful is a clever way to solve problems, yet, it's solution-focused—no sense dwelling in the land of what we can't change. In order to make the word resourceful a part of your armor, or a feather in your cap—whichever you prefer—here are three quick ideas:

1. By naming yourself resourceful, you are creating a powerful new affirmation that stamps out the weaker negative thoughts floating around your head. Affirm, "I am resourceful!" But if you add the three words, "*I trust that* I am resourceful," you have just strengthened the statement.

Say it out loud three times in front of the mirror. Notice how you stand taller, breathe more deeply and feel like you're ready to take on the world.

2. After you have affirmed resourcefulness, stop a moment to consider the matter at hand and notice how your thinking becomes clearer. You are free to relax, knowing that each question you ask has an answer waiting to be captured. Use your imagination or your favorite meditation exercise to picture yourself climbing the stairs toward the answer. Perceptive thoughts are a part of your nature. Use them.

3. No matter what challenge comes your way, you have the "right stuff" to find it, fix it or take it out of your life. It might be something you can take care of yourself or you may wish to enlist the help of others. After all, your friends are an important resource. Reach within to find confidence in your rock-solid core.

From my book *Rock Solid Confidence,* let me add, "We know we're doing well when we feel anticipation for each day because we believe that whatever curve ball is thrown our way, we'll be able to handle it. When we feel insecure, we calmly notice the feeling, and use the tools we have learned to keep us on a steady path of growth."

This magic word *Resourceful* will see you through many

trials and tests. Use it to transform your stumbling blocks into a stairway to success!

Your Conversation Questions:

Laura Thomas lives in Alaska, yet as a Peace Corps volunteer, she called Botswana her home for a few years. Being a wife and mom has also broadened her perspective and strengthened her resourcefulness. Here are her suggested questions:

1. Have you ever found yourself in a situation where you had to be resourceful? Explain.

2. As humans, we are interdependent. Who are your "go to" people when you need assistance?

3. When Laura went into the hospital for a medical procedure, her friend told her, "If anyone can get through this, I know you can." How might the right words spoken at the right time affect a you?

4. How have you helped someone in your life have a more positive outlook on life?

5. Name three successes from your past? How can listing your successes help you manage your future?

6. When thinking about a movie, which leading lady (or man) embodies the characteristics you would like to emulate?

7. Have you ever had a great idea for a project that was difficult, but by being resourceful, you pulled it off? Explain.

9.

DISCOVERING YOUR STRIDE OF

CONFIDENCE

Confidence is something most people crave. Confidence is an illusive character who resides in the mind, yet there are specific ways to show it and grow it. The other day while unpacking my books, I came across a book of poems by several college students, including my gifted nephew, Eric Whalen.

While looking through the book, the poem "Confidence" caught my eye. As luck would have it, Eric was its author and gave me permission to share part of it with you. When you read his words, think of the most confident woman you know:

> When she walked, she swung her arms wide, out and away from her body and they rotated like dual pendulums. Keeping her forward motion moving, and so a large area of space suspended around her body which no body could penetrate....she stepped definitely on purposefully chosen patches of ground in front of her, reserved for her feet. Determination in any direction and you made no mistake guessing which way she was going...

Eric captured perfectly the way a confident woman moves forward with purpose, and takes HER space on the path with neither anger nor apology. The vividness of Eric's poem reminds me of the day my voice coach, the late Dr. Ralph Hillman told me to stand up and walk for him. *Walk? What does that have to do with my voice?* What he could see, but I didn't know yet, was my "potential" for walking with more confidence and why it was important to me.

Here is a typical lesson from Dr. Hillman, **the Voice Doc.** In his own words, he shares three exercises he developed to build confidence with his university students:

1. "Walk thirty (30) steps using **short steps**. On a sheet of paper, write how you feel. Turn that paper over. Then, walk thirty (30) steps using **long strides**, stretching to make them even longer. Now write how you feel and compare notes."

Did you feel the difference? The small steps remind me of the way Chinese women of the past, with bound feet, were forced to walk. We are fortunate to be living in a different time and place, but for some reason, many of us don't access our full walking potential.

2. "Sit at a table with shoulders rolled forward for a minute or two. Take pen in hand and write down how you feel right now. When finished writing, turn that piece of paper over. A few minutes later while seated, pull your shoulders back and straighten your back; now write on another sheet of paper how you feel. Compare your notes."

3. "Early in the morning with pen and paper ready, as you put your feet on the floor, in a soft breathy voice say: 'Today is going to be a great day!' You may need to repeat this a couple of times. Write how you feel. Crawl back into bed and get out again. As your feet hit the floor in a strong, loud voice say: 'Today is going to be a great day!' Write how you feel and compare notes."

Dr. Hillman explains: "In the first instance with your posture, stride and voice quality, your actions are giving information to your body and brain. Words like *hesitant, unsure, passive, pessimistic,* are very real in describing how you feel about yourself.

"In the second instance of each of the posture, stride, and voice quality exercises words like *strength, eagerness, courage, optimistic* are more likely to come to mind. These kinds of messages to your body and brain give you confidence."

Based on your own experience with these exercises, do you agree? You may be interested in knowing that all ten of his voice qualities are described in his book, *Delivering Dynamic Presentations.*

I've discovered, through my own self-exploration and working as a presentation coach, it is possible to unknowingly pick up habits that erode confidence, but we file them under a category we call, "This-is-just-the-way-I-am," not realizing that each of us can make a different choice.

I invite you to experiment with the strength of your voice, posture and stride in everyday life and watch your confidence grow. Be the woman in Eric's poem who steps purposefully knowing exactly which way you're going.

Your Conversation Questions:

Ellen Whalen is a busy woman. She's an assistant editor for *The Fillmore County Journal*; a valued member of the team, and always learning more about the various aspects of the business. She also owns and works on her family farm near Harmony, Minnesota. She makes time for friends and fun, and brings joy to her children (Eric is one of her four children) and grandchildren. She suggests these discussion questions:

1. Do you ever think about your level of confidence, or is it something that never occurs to you?

2. Who is the most confident woman you know? What is it about her that makes her seem confident?

3. When have you felt you were walking (moving) as a very confident person? Why were you moving confidently?

4. Think about whether you agree or disagree with this statement: If you purposefully put yourself into each moment, you'll be more effective and happy with what you're doing. Explain.

5. Is your confidence level affected by how other people approach you? For example, if someone says, "You're good at this and ….." Or if they say, "I don't know if you can do this, but…." Are you more or less likely to do it?

6. Name something you'll be doing in the near future where you'll be more effective if your voice, tone and posture express confidence.

10.

PROMISES TO KEEP

Part of personal confidence comes from knowing that we follow through on our promises. When we set a goal and achieve it, confidence increases. When we set a goal and forget it or don't give it our full effort, confidence and trust fall over the cliff.

Keeping promises builds trust and the hardest promises to keep, in my opinion, are the ones we make to ourselves. We make promises about losing weight, about cleaning the office, or calling friends on a regular basis. Another year goes by and we see no progress. Here's a personal example:

Just recently, I decided to set a goal to write an uplifting letter to one friend or relative each day. I felt good, imagining the joy they'd receive, but then days went by and no letters were written. Nice goal, easy goal, but my inaction motivated my inner-critic to shout nasty things to me—words I don't want to repeat here—but I'm sure you get the picture.

This went on for quite a few days until I realized that it was time for action. Action is a great confidence builder. Hope returned as I sat down to write twenty-one notes in two sittings. It gave me a new attitude about myself, one of accomplishment. More importantly, the action boosted my self-trust.

Action proves that we can keep commitments, and then our discipline becomes a habit. As a result, we are ready to tackle other tasks and goals we've put off. Confidence is a spiral. We humans are either stepping out of our comfort zones, trying new things, acting on goals or not—spiraling up or spiraling down. There's not much in between.

So what are you thinking about doing?

Is there something your inner critic harps about that you CAN do something about? Start small. Choose one doable task and step-by-step, the voice that loves to praise you will overshadow all the nasty voices in your head.

Go for it!

Your Conversation questions:

Betty Johnson is a champion of service, reaching every segment of the community in Cedar Rapids, Iowa. She has devoted her life to drug and alcohol abuse counseling, prevention of violence in the workplace, and economic disparities of the under-served. She's an inspiring leader, to say the least. Here are her suggested discussion questions:

1. Do you make New Years resolutions? If you make them, do you keep them? Explain.

2. A promise is like an unwritten contract. Is it easier for you to keep promises to yourself or to others? Why?

3. Which voice in your head gets more of your attention: 1.The "inner critic," or 2. The "inner cheerleader"? Why do you think this is so?

4. How does it feel when you make a promise to yourself and keep it? Describe that feeling of satisfaction.

5. What is a good way to be more accountable and more faithful to yourself in keeping your promises?

6. Based on your many years of living, what is the correlation between keeping promises and maintaining your confidence?

11.

THE SPIRITUAL ANCHOR OF CONFIDENCE

The confidence we experience as we walk through each day is a multifaceted phenomenon. We visualize dancing, skipping and breezing from one moment to the next, but truth be told, some days feel more like trudging through mud. Sure, self-worth is a factor of knowing your value to the world. Your family of origin and the others you've attracted into your life also affect your confidence and, to some extent, help you maintain your sense of belief in yourself.

There's one more foundational key in this secret confidence triad: your spiritual anchor. The old saying goes, "There are no atheists in foxholes." When things get tough, we turn to something or someone beyond ourselves and the people we know. We search for a Supreme Being that will be our rock, our anchor—no matter which storm rages around us.

For the past two decades, as a presentation coach, I always inquired about the client's spiritual beliefs in order to know how to assist them in anchoring their confidence. I believe that if we want to successfully reach the core of confidence, we need to dive into this topic.

Contrary to contemporary lingo, one can be both

religious and spiritual. Organized religion offers a connection to Divine strength and opportunities for fellowship and caring. I imagine God putting words into people's minds and mouths to comfort and heal: "Call Joyce today." "Tell that girl she's wise to wait for a guy who appreciates her." "Tell her, 'You know your mom was proud of you. She always bragged about your determination.'"

Words read from scripture (no matter what you call your holy book) can make a great impact on your spirit. I recently asked a friend how her religious beliefs helped her cope with her husband's cancer. Without missing a beat, she answered, "I just don't know how I could get through the day without it."

Many find the Divine in nature, music and art. The presence of organic beauty reminds us that we are all a part of the great plan. In quiet moments, comfort overtakes us, supports us, whispers to us. Signs of the Divine come through the wind, the words of a song, or the innocent question of a child.

Meditation and yoga have become very popular with people from all walks of life, and why not? Praying is talking to God and meditation is a way to listen. Isn't it about time we stopped the mind chatter, worry and fear in order to listen?

An Apache proverb tells us: "It makes no difference as to the name of the God, since love is the real God of all the world."

I also like what Albert Einstein said: "When you examine the lives of the most influential people who have ever walked among us, you discover one thread that winds through them all. They have been aligned first with their spiritual nature and only then with their physical selves."

The foundation of your confidence is a triad. You reach

in to find worth; reach out to those around you for support and validation; and reach up to the Divine source of life. Like a grand secret, all three keys of this triad are connected.

Confidence is multifaceted, yet, with this powerful triad of self, others and Spirit, we are able to withstand any of life's storms.

Your Conversation Questions:

Glenda Myers is a rare individual who is loved by many for her unbridled enthusiasm and warmth. A former hospice nurse, writer and storyteller, she has personally encouraged me to help others write their stories. Here are her discussion questions:

1. The term "Spiritual Anchor" has been used. What are other names given to the spiritual source? Examples: The Divine, Supreme Being.

2. Quoting Scripture, according to one's own religion can bring comfort in times of need. What are two or three passages you quote that bring strength and comfort to you?

3. How do your spiritual beliefs affect your choices in life?

4. How can a spiritual anchor help you in times of trauma, stress or during transitions?

5. What other paths or groups (besides belonging to a church) have people joined to come together for a cause greater than themselves? Can this be a spiritual anchor? Why or why not? Example: animal rescue groups, environmental groups.

6. How does your spiritual anchor affect your confidence?

12.

COURAGE DRIVES ACTION

These are interesting times, wouldn't you say? Days can be challenging, uncertain and more than once in a week, we may find ourselves immobilized by an insurmountable problem—or so it seems. However, this isn't our first rodeo. We are souls who know danger, yet step up. Courage is the force within us that keeps us moving forward *anyway*.

Courage is what sustains us as we reach for our goals and can be found in many places:

- Caregivers tirelessly care for the needs of dementia patients

- Activists advocate for a cause

- The abused woman sets out on her own to make a better life for herself and her children

- The non-traditional student returns to school after years in the work force

- A 50-something woman seeks a new job where she is valued

Man's Search for Meaning is a famous and often quoted book by Victor Frankl. Whenever I feel like hiding in a corner, or taking a long nap to avoid some mundane problem I face, Frankl brings me back to the reality that we humans are stronger than we think, and by facing our individual challenges—we are fulfilling our purpose in being here.

Each day is new and each decision is personal. Frankl says this with eloquence:

> Life does not mean something vague, but something very real and concrete, just as life's tasks are also very real and concrete. They form man's destiny, which is different and unique for each individual. No man and no destiny can be compared with any other man or any other destiny. No situation repeats itself, and each situation calls for a different response.

Courage drives *action*. To activate our courage, we need to step outside our comfort zone. We need to chose that forward movement even though we know we could fail. Step by step we proceed. We are fueled by Hope, and grounded by the triad of Self-Worth, Family Support and our Spiritual Anchor. We press forward, using the past as a guide.

Trust your intuition. Get up. Move on. Step forward. Touch your shining star.

Your Conversation Questions:

Karen Needham has been described as "a party in a box" due to her unique way of mixing fun with practical problem solving. She's the Director of Orchestra Operations for Virtuosi of Houston, mother of three, and a "Glam-ma" to her grandchildren. Here are her discussion questions:

1. Have you ever witnessed someone courageously stepping out of their comfort zone to become successful?

2. Give an example of a time when you stepped out of your comfort zone. What goal had you set for yourself? Did you accomplish your goal?

3. What signs might show up in your life to let you know that it is time for you to take a risk and step out of your comfort zone?

4. A baby does not know how to walk. He/she needs to be helped through the process. Have you ever encouraged or mentored someone to take their first steps in a new direction? Explain.

5. Thinking about someone who is in your life today, how might you support and encourage them to follow their dreams?

FRIENDSHIP

"Real friendship or love is not manufactured or achieved by an act of will or intention. Friendship is always an act of recognition."

~John O'Donohue,
Anam Cara: A Book of Celtic Wisdom

13.

FIVE FRIENDS WHO ENRICH YOUR LIFE

Who are the five friends making a difference in your life? Count them:

1. **Your Long-Time Friend.** Think of the woman you have known for many years. She's been with you for the big moments of your life's journey: births, deaths, graduations, marriages, joys, tears—all of it. No matter how many years (or decades) pass, when you get back together, it feels as if no time has passed. You might even say, "Seeing you again makes me remember why I've always liked you so much."

Who comes to mind?

2. **Your New Friend.** This new friend affirms that the world is teeming with interesting people—and you've just met one more. Trading stories and sharing what's the same and different gives you another perspective of yourself and the world. We all like something new, and discovering a new friend is better than finding a great new pair of shoes.

What is his or her name?

3. **Your Younger Friend**. She hasn't lived as long as you, but she knows things you don't because she inhabits a different generation. She brings fresh ideas, optimism and a nostalgic innocence. You delight in her big dreams and share in her successes. And she teaches you cool stuff.

Can you think of someone like this?

4. **Your Well-Seasoned Friend.** Yes, she's lived more years than you, but somehow, you share the same vibe. You notice a common track in the way you think and feel. She has been where you will go (God willing you get to live that long) and you cherish her wisdom. You wish you could sit at her feet to listen to her stories, amazed by her resilience.

Are you lucky enough to know such a woman or man?

5. **Your Relative Friend.** You can't pick your relatives, but sometimes you get lucky and feel the connection of friendship with a woman in your family. She may be older or younger, but that doesn't matter because you share a heritage—a family that may be rocky or stable. She's a woman to validate you and together, you navigate the family tree.

What name comes to mind?

I've made my list. I invite you to make your own. I'll not be surprised if you have more than one woman in some of the categories. Lucky you!

Now, tell them. Make sure they know how their lives have blessed yours. Don't wait for Thanksgiving. NOW is the best time to "gift" them with the truth of their value to you.

Your Conversation questions:

Sherry Munther, from Missoula, Montana, is everyone's friend extraordinaire—collects and nurtures friendships wherever she goes. She has friends from her working days, her golf team, two book clubs, Kiwanis club, from Arizona as a winter visitor, and all parts in between. She realizes that friendships ebb and flow, yet make her world go round. Here are Sherry's questions:

1. When thinking about your friends, which categories bring up the most friends? Which type of friends are the easiest to name? The hardest?

2. Throughout your life, where have you met the most friends?

3. Have any of your friendships changed, either positively or negatively, in the past few years? Explain why you think this happened.

4. Do you have a friendship that seems to be one sided—you contact them, but they don't reciprocate? How do you feel about that?

5. We all experience life's ups and downs, yet does a constant negative attitude ever affect your friendships?

6. What part does humor play in your friendships?

7. How can feedback and conversations with friends who have different opinions about various subjects help us grow?

14.

DO FRIENDS GIVE YOU CONFIDENCE?

As a part of International Woman's Day, I reposted two versions of a familiar statement on my Facebook page: "Behind every successful woman is another woman." By inserting "man" it could also be true. The second states, "Behind every successful woman is herself."

So which is it? Self or others? Is our success, or confidence, based on ourselves alone or do others play a role? As simple as this sounds, we need to start living as if both have value.

The truth is, we need self-esteem, self-worth and all those other self-hyphenated words we see in the dictionary in order to walk confidently into the day. And it's equally true that we can't make it through this life alone. Even Batman, in *The Lego Batman Movie*, discovered the need for friends and family. If a super hero needs his peeps, regular people certainly benefit from a crew, a team, or a tribe.

The dichotomy of self-reliance and dependence was demonstrated to me long ago when our family moved to a farm in Iowa. As city kids, we didn't know much about animals, life or the benefits of struggle. When the first baby chicks were ready to hatch, we got excited about the miracle of chicken birth.

If you're not from the farm, let me explain the process of how the eggs hatch. First comes a tapping sound from the inside of the egg (pipping), and you see bits of shell crack and lift; the egg moves. The chick is really working to get out of that confined space. This goes on for up to 24 hours. When she finally escapes, she's a curled-up wet mess.

The Whalens are world-class "helpers," so my brother, Len, and I "helped" a chick by removing bits of shell. We didn't know that survival *needs* struggle. Maybe the old saying, "Whatever doesn't kill you makes you stronger," refers to this oddity of nature.

Yet struggle isn't an odd event. It's the normal way of the world. What if struggle, any struggle, is an initiation ceremony to build strength and prepare us for the life ahead.

A successful independent birth leaves the chick dry, fluffy and looking for its family. Just like us, its family can be the flesh and blood relatives or others who nurture us. Science classifies family as those with significant shared characteristics. How many times have we told someone close to us, "You're just like family"?

It didn't take Scott, my youngest son, long to feel comfortable in his new state when he started school at ASU in Tempe, Arizona. I joked that he had "found his tribe," and when I saw pictures of him with his new group of friends, they all looked like brothers.

When reflecting about the family you started with, you might have some regrets. They say, "It's hard to get over a good start—or a bad one." I'm not sure that's completely true because we all know people who are successful in spite of, (and maybe because of) the struggles they had growing up. Yet it's possible to break out of that shell and thrive.

We have a lot in common with those newborn chicks. We each need to be independent enough to come out of our own shell, and also give and receive support from each other. This interdependence gives us a strong foundation for happiness.

Your Conversation Questions

Karen Bahti is gifted at quilting, sewing, cooking and friendship. The warmth of her Patagonia, Arizona home represents quintessential Christian hospitality. She's a wife, mother and grandmother. Here are Karen's suggested questions:

1. Time is a valuable commodity; we only have 24 hours each day. What type of people do you choose to spend your time with? Explain why.

2. "Grief shared lightens your burden and joy shared doubles your joy." What experiences come to mind about sharing your grief and joy with your friends?

3. What are the benefits of having family members who also seem like friends?

4. It seems as if our lives spin round and round, but when we experience an illness or a loss, the spinning twists us, pulling us off-kilter. How might our friends assist in bringing us into balance once more? Give examples from your life.

5. Creating something (art, writing, painting, building) has the power to uplift our spirits. Sometimes we create alone, and other times we create together. What do you like to create with others or for others?

15.

A TRUE FRIEND: SEVEN CHARACTERISTICS

Let's count the ways your friends support you.

COMPANIONSHIP: Together is better. Companionship is a personal connection you have with someone to share the joy and divide the load. This is the person who will go with you to a movie, conference, shopping trip, or golf outing. Some jobs are better when two heads work together, rather than alone.

INTEGRITY: Deliver the truth. Most people don't care enough about you to tell you that your eye shadow is old fashioned or you've gotten a bit negative lately. The relationship is strong enough to withstand unpleasant conversations, especially if messages are given with a tone of kindness.

OPTIMISM: Tell you the ideal truth. After trying something new, like a dance, a musical instrument or a new speech, it's lovely to have someone in your corner say, "I am so proud of you!" In your heart you know you could have done better, yet sometimes hearing the raw truth, when you're just a beginner, can devastate your desire to get back on the horse. Yes, this kind of truth is the opposite of integrity; yet I've found that there are legitimate times when a full evaluation does not set you free; it robs you of future competence and confidence.

SUPPORT: Lend you a hand, money or advice. Think of those taxing jobs, the kind that you can't even pay some one to do, or you're too broke to pay for yourself. Supportive friends give you what you need. Family and those like family step forward when others step back. They want you to know you're not alone. They care about you and your success.

LOYALTY: Take your side. In a confrontation or a fight,between you and someone else, your tribe takes your side. Sometimes they also take you aside to ask what in the heck you were thinking, but even squabbling siblings and true friends faithfully stay on your team during difficulties. Even if you do something really bad, loyal friends might say, "I'm sure she had a good reason for her actions."

DISCRETION: Keep your secrets. Because of your history together, your people know and safeguard the things you don't want to share with the world. Trust has been built to a point of knowing that your confession will go no further than that person's ears. It's wonderful to have this space for safe honesty.

UNCONDITIONAL LOVE: Love is always there. Time and space may separate you, yet you can be confident of this unbreakable foundation you share. It's not dependent upon any event or circumstance of life. This bond gives you the assurance that you are safe, solid and secure. With it, the rest feels insignificant.

No wonder we crave these relationships. It doesn't matter how long you have been friends, or even if those who play the friend role are actually family (double bonus), they are foundational to living a healthy life.

Your Conversation Questions:

Julie Crooks, is a human resource specialist with a quick smile and peaceful energy. She's gained wisdom from a background in a variety of work environments. Julie has also written a fascinating book about healing, based upon the rather harsh circumstances of her youth. She suggests these discussion questions:

1. How have *you* been a friend? Select the top three characteristics that express your strengths as a friend.

2. When you think of your best friends, what characteristics are they most likely to have?

3. How can these characteristics translate to work relationships?

4. Have you experienced the reverse of these characteristics? If so, how has that affected your life?

BONUS GROUP OPTION:

Divide those in attendance into three sub-groups. Assign the following characteristic:

- Companionship - Unconditional Love
- Integrity - Optimism - Discretion
- Support - Loyalty

Each sub-group will discuss:

- Define each of the characteristics you've been given.
- How are these characteristics similar? Different?
- Give examples from your life where your friends displayed these characteristics.
- Give examples from your life where friends DID NOT display these characteristics.

If time allows, share your sub-group discussions with the entire group.

16.

CHAR'S THREE ROOTS OF WISDOM

We have a million reasons to love our friends: they understand us, they support us, and they know just what to say when we're having an off day. Through the years my friends have helped me understand that there is always a new day and a new way to look at a bleak situation.

I'd like you to meet Char, one of those friends. Her words are roots of wisdom because they have the power to ground us, bring us back to a place where we can think clearly and make decisions about what to do. I've heard these words on some of my darkest days, so I know they work.

Here is her first piece of advice: Imagine you are in the middle of a sticky situation with someone you don't know very well. You wonder, *Is this person telling the truth? Are they exaggerating?* You really want to get to the bottom of it but feel stuck. Char looks at you with a knowing grin and says, **"...and more will be revealed."**

When she says this, you remember that life is a process. Events and personalities unfold naturally. Yes, love at first sight is real (and often temporary), but time has a way of revealing other sides of a personality or situation. Sooner or later, if you pay attention, things will become clear.

Here is Char's second bit of wisdom. You've made a

major change and are planning a new life. Your head is overloaded with all the things that need to happen. Your mind creates a list that grows and grows until you're so confused, you want to forget the whole thing. Char knows how you feel, hands you a cup of tea and says, **"You don't have to figure it ALL out right now."**

If you're like me, you sigh, because she's right. "Rome wasn't built in a day," and her words give you permission to rest; metaphorically lifting a cement ball off your back. It's okay to admit you don't know all the steps. All you have to do is begin at a logical starting point. Take the next reasonable step and then the next. When I'm especially frustrated, I also remind myself that the project is not infinite. It might be big, but given enough time and energy—it will end.

The third root helps when negative thoughts take over. Let's say you have been asked to give a speech in front of your peers on a topic you don't know very well. You hate public speaking and dread this event. You might say something like this, "I'm not a speaker. I don't like to get up in front of my peers, and besides, some of them know more about the topic than I do. I'll probably embarrass myself."

Char would encourage you to get these negative feelings out into the open—no use letting them grow into an ugly mess inside your body, giving you a migraine or indigestion. But at some point, expect her to call for the question: **"So what is your new story?"**

At that point you will need to close down your pity-party and affirm *what you wish to be true*. You begin your *new story* like this: "In the past, I have not enjoyed speaking to groups, yet my boss must have faith in me, or I wouldn't have been asked to speak. I am willing to give an interesting and informative presentation and I look forward to the benefits this opportunity brings."

Char will tell you that the new story is a way to shape your future. The old story has been chipping away at your foundation and your confidence; while the new story brings positive words that support positive feelings. With enough "new stories" you strengthen the roots that are necessary to hold you steady during the storms ahead.

Seasoned friends can be the best teachers. They give sage advice based on their own life experiences. This shared wisdom anchors our lives.

Your Conversation Questions:
Adrienne McGill is an award winning multi-passionate entrepreneur. She successfully transitioned a 20 year corporate career in the insurance industry to founding a high end boutique in the Chicago suburbs to coaching entrepreneurs. She now lives in Arizona with her husband and enjoys spoiling the new loves of her life: two adorable kittens. Here are her suggested discussion questions:

1. What words of wisdom have *you* received in your life?

2. Do you consider yourself wise? Why or why not?

3. Looking back on your life, was there ever a time when

you didn't feel you had it all figured out, but it worked out better than you expected?

4. What stories did you tell yourself in the past that are no longer true? What stories do you tell yourself now that need to change?

5. Has your first impression of someone you've met been totally wrong? How so?

6. Have you ever been in a situation that seemed foggy but as time went on, things got clear? Explain.

7. Have you ever known that something was wrong with your relationship with your friend, but you didn't "pay attention" to your intuition? What was the result?

17.

Have you ever noticed that events seem to come in threes? This might be the way the Divine gets our attention. My trio of recent events involved two visits from friends from my past and the unfortunate passing of a third friend. Through these meetings, and especially through the lens of our earthly mortality, we pay attention to life more closely.

So what is a life? We begin our solitary journey as a helpless infant (hopefully with a supportive cast of players), we get curious about the world as a child, and if we are lucky, we keep on living. We live our days with ups and downs, but at some point, we leave our body behind.

As we walk through life, we're accompanied by a variety of characters; some hang out with us for a short time, and some become lifelong friends—each vital to our growth and happiness.

Even though we know that life is temporary, when we're with someone, we have a tendency to take them for granted. I don't know about you, but I sometimes find my mind wandering elsewhere—not hearing or seeing my friend, but rather wrapped up in my own daily drama. I fritter away my time with them as if they will be with me forever.

The following are seven reminders to lead us into a place of being more attentive to others:

1. In the presence of others, make it a general practice to put the phone (or other devises) away in order to see and

hear them. Research tells us that it's impossible to multi-task, so turn the focus on them. Grab your coffee, relax and smile to encourage them to open up.

2. Set aside judgment and get curiosity about their stories. Ask questions to make sure you see life from their point of view, and avoid accusatory questions or advice (unless asked).

3. Make a list of individuals you want to call, write or email just to keep in touch. Set a schedule for following through—maybe two a week. Chances are, the older you are, the larger the list. Be sure to tell them how they have affected your life, or what good they have done for the world.

4. Make a list of everyone you've said, "We need to get together sometime." Make the time rather than wait for a perfect time. Set a date.

5. If someone's name comes to mind, for any reason and especially if you remember how influential they have been in your life, contact them as soon as possible. If it's 3am, write a note to yourself so you don't forget.

6. Reconcile with anyone you're not on good terms with—even if it's an email or letter. You might say, "I'm sad that we are not on the best of terms now. I want you to know that you are important to me." My brother gives a gift to people in this category because it transforms his attitude about them.

7. When parting, treat the departure with reverence and regard. Our journey seems eternal, yet it's only temporary.

By acting on a few of the suggestions on this list, you will not only feel more connected to your friends, you'll be building self-trust by keeping promises to yourself.

Your Conversation Questions:

Deb Frese is an organizer of gatherings, a mother of four children, and a loyal friend who realizes that balancing family, work and friend-gatherings keep her saying, "Oh joy!" She feels that life is too short to hope someone calls her; she takes action. Here are her suggested discussion questions:

1. Deb remembers a friend who was overtaken with Alzheimer's. In our busy world, it's easy to think our friends will be here forever. Name three friends you'd like to make sure you contact this week? Explain.

2. Well Seasoned women have friends in many categories. For example: high school friends, college friends, neighborhood friends. Name 5 categories of friends from the different "seasons" of your life.

3. Throughout our lives, friends come and go. What types of life circumstances (clubs, groups, children's activities, volunteer and work situations) are responsible for *your* friends to appear or move away from your life?

4. Among your group of friends, who usually organizes activities? Is it you, or someone else? Why do you think this is so?

5. Imagine that you are in charge of planning a day of fun for a small group of your friends. Money is no object. Describe that day.

6. What are your main reasons for reaching out to your friends—either by phone or in person?

18.

REACH OUT TO BLESS

I've always loved the words: "When you're down, reach up; when you're up, reach down." This phrase reflects the fact that we need each other. We need each other because we all experience both the mountain-top and dark-valley days of life—and it can be lonely at the top and the bottom (and in between too).

We have many opportunities to be of service, to BLESS those who cross our path: our kids, parents, siblings, teachers, co-workers, neighbors, the clerk at the post office, the parking lot attendant. But as busy as life is, how do we squeeze one more thing into the schedule?

Blessing others can mean many things and you'll find dozens of Biblical references for the word bless, yet I like to think of it as simply paying attention to the actions and the good intentions of others—and then letting them know you "see them," to quote a line in the movie *Avatar*.

In *Avatar*, the Na'vi blessing "I see you," is relatable because of its double meaning. First of all, it means that my eyes physically see *you*—you exist in my mind. Secondly, I connect with you, thank you and appreciate the role you play in the world.

We can't go around saying, "I see you" to every person we meet (although when the movie came out, some people did), but we can bless others by getting specific about what we see in them. This feedback is vital because most of us don't know how we affect others, and as we all know, it's easy to get discouraged from the bumps and disappointments of everyday life.

Here are a few fill-in-the-blanks (and some examples) for you to adapt to BLESS those in your world:

- "What I like about you is…" (you always look at the bright side of a problem).

- "What I like about you is your…" (on-point analysis of my report).

- "You always know how to…." (bring humor into a tense situation).

- "You always make me feel ___when you…" (valued when you take notes as I speak).

- You probably don't realize this but you …." (are the only person I trust with my secrets).

- "Most people would not notice this, but I see…" (the way you quietly mentor all of us).

- "I'm proud of you. You…" (have not always had the easiest life, but you exude joy).

- "You're a good example of someone who…" (knows how to forgive and move on).

- "When I see (hear/read) your work I know…" (you care deeply about others).

- "Keep doing what you're doing because it is…" (such a great example for the rest of us).

We have a responsibility to show up and to bless others. But who? I remember the words of the character Dharma, in the 90s television comedy show *Dharma and Greg.* In the show Dharma, a freedom loving yoga instructor who grew up with hippy parents, was continuously trying to help others. One day Greg, her somewhat-stuffy lawyer husband, spoke up. "Dharma, you can't save everyone in the whole world."

"Yes, I know," she answered, "but what about the one standing right in front of me?"

Thanks, Dharma. Let's promise to look around at who is in front of us today. My intension is to see them, and reach out to affirm their dignity and worth.

Your Conversation Questions:

Nicole Kronebusch, a nurse serving in the Air Force, feels that to be blessed is to be complete, uplifted and thankful. She invests in people by being present to them, giving her time and attention. She likes to bring out the best in each person she speak with by asking questions to get them to think about their life. Nicole suggests these discussion questions:

1. What is your definition of being blessed?

2. Nicole says, "It is not healthy to do it on your own. We are meant to be in community." Do you agree or disagree with this statement. Why?

3. Even strong and independent women need others. Was there ever a point in your life where you didn't think you needed anyone, but then an event caused you to realize we are all interdependent? Explain.

4. Paying attention to others validates and connects us to them. Our input lets them know they matter to us, and keeps loneliness away. Has social media changed how we "see" people?

5. Friendship has a language. Many affirmations have been mentioned in this chapter. Time, gifts and expression of affection are ways to show friendship. How do you like to show your friends you appreciate them?

6. Many times we can see strengths and talents in our friends that they do not see in themselves. However, until they see their own potential, our opinions of them are ineffective. How do you help somebody reach their best self, yet still maintain healthy boundaries?

19.

DECIDING TO CHOOSE

Imagine getting a call from a friend. She tells you about her frustration at work and wants to quit, then asks, "What should I do?" Unlike the Super Bowl where you have several referees, line judges and armchair quarterbacks to determine the outcome, our personal decisions are not always clear cut.

Making decisions is a part of life even though I've heard myself say, "I didn't have a choice." The average adult makes up to 35,000 decisions each day. No wonder we're so tired.

In Ruth Chang's TED talk, "How to Make Hard Choices," she divides choices into two categories: easy and hard. With an easy choice, one result is clearly better than the other: Would I like fresh coffee or stale coffee? A no-brainer.

She contrasts this with a hard choice, where each option has some positives, some drawbacks and some unknowns: Should I keep my house in the country where it is peaceful or move to the city so I can be closer to the theater?

Ironically, with so many ways to look at decision making, I had a difficult time deciding where to begin, so I'm going to share these five amazing quotes about choice:

- *"Our lives are a sum total of the choices we have*

made." In this statement, Wayne Dyer eludes to the domino effect of each step we take. If you had made another choice, that choice would have led you down a different path, maybe a different life. "What if..." thinking can bring unnecessary regret. Sure, you could have married Ron Kennedy, instead of Tom Nixon, but you may be trading problem A for problems B, C and D.

- *"It is our choices...that show what we truly are, far more than our abilities."* Was J. K. Rowling comparing high school transcripts with real life accomplishments? We love movies because they are stories about life as it is or could be, reflected on the big screen. We are inspired by the courageous choices our favorite movie characters make when they: give up a child so she'll have a better life, travel to a strange land in search of a lost friend, brave the elements to get back home—the list goes on. To witness ordinary people taking action gives a better example for living than brainy people who sit around weighing options.

- *"When people have too many choices, they make bad choices."* Yes, scientist Thom Browne reports that our society burdens us with so many options, we're paralyzed. When we get to the coffee shop, we need to decide: hot? cold? caf? decaf? skim? soy? whipped cream (why not?). A seasoned customer simplifies life by ordering the same beverage each time. According to Sheena Lyengar, three things happen when we have too many choices: 1. we procrastinate, making no choice; 2. we worry about the choice; 3. we regret the choice. Costco embraces the philosophy of less is more by offering fewer options. If you're in their store looking for a bathroom scale, you can buy scale #1 or scale #2—and statistically, with only two choices, we usually make a purchase. When my son Mike was two, I used the same strategy. I'd say, "Do you want to sit on the right side of the car or the left side?" This trick worked perfectly until he turned three, when he decided he really didn't want to get into the car at all.

- *"A real decision is measured by the fact that you've taken a new action. If there's no action, you haven't truly decided."* Tony Robbins reminds us that action is important in committing to our plans. Personally, I feel an upcoming vacation is real only after I've made the plane reservations. With that step, I have a clear direction. Action expands confidence. In my book *Rock Solid Confidence*, you'll read:

Confidence is the self-assurance and boldness we posses to make decisions, take risks, ask for what we want, feel sure of what we're doing and live with zest.

- *"Bad decisions make good stories"* is a funny line by Ellis Vidler, that reminds us that sometimes we make too much of our decisions. In the mid 90s I coached speakers and also gave many presentations. Once in a while my client would (half jokingly) say that they'd be judging my speech. In order to relieve the pressure to be perfect, I'd tell myself, *This will either be good or I can use it as a good example of what not to do.* (I don't like waste.) It helped me through each event. When you write the story of your life, make sure you include bad decisions because they not only make good stories, they celebrate your courage, perseverance and problem-solving skills.

At the end of the day, when a friend asks what she should do, sometimes it's helpful to have a stack of tried and true sayings. Sometimes it's appropriate to go over the pros and cons of each option; yet she may not really be asking for your wisdom at all.

She may simply need a safe place and an open heart to tell the facts, unpack her conflicting thoughts, and sort her emotions. It takes maturity and finesse to be a true friend without blurting out what *you* would do. Support her with Lee Ann Womack lyrics, "And when you get the choice to sit it out or dance, I hope you dance."

And if that doesn't work, you can always flip a coin.

Your Conversation Questions:

Dar Schlicht and Jerri Thomas have been friends for many years at Perryville. Their letters to me are filled with dreams of one day gaining the freedom to own a dog, have coffee at a coffee shop, or wander in the woods. They have lead Bible studies and classes—coaching others to live their best life, no matter what set of circumstance brought them to prison. Here are their suggested discussion questions:

1. Are choices usually easy or difficult for you to make?

2. Which author's quote most closely reflects your own thinking about choices: Wayne Dyer, J.K. Rowling, Thom Browne, Tony Robbins, Ellis Vidler? Explain.

3. We all make choices we regret. Name a choice you regretted at first, but later that choice led to a positive result.

4. What is the relationship between choices and wisdom?

5. Read the following three scenarios and choose what you would do. Answer questions A, B and C as accurately as possible. At the end, evaluate your responses.

A. You are in a meeting with your peers and a leader is needed for a new project. You would:

a. be the first person to volunteer

b. request more information on the project

c. ask if bonus pay is included

d. suggest another person for the position

B. You are the first person at the scene of a traffic accident with someone trapped in the vehicle. You would:

a. call police for assistance

b. run to the car to see if the trapped person is hurt

c. drive on

d. take charge of the area by directing traffic away from the scene

C. You are knee-deep in work and you receive a call from your spouse informing you that your six-year-old just broke her arm. You would:

a. tell your spouse to handle the situation, you cannot leave the office

b. drop everything and get home to handle the child's trauma

c. give specific directions to your spouse expecting them to be followed

d. panic

Do you see a pattern in your choices? Are you more of a risk taker, someone who requires lots of information, one who considers the impact on others, looking for a win-win?

WRITING

"*Across the millennia, an author is speaking clearly and silently inside your head, directly to you. Writing is perhaps the greatest of human inventions, binding together people who never knew each other, citizens of distant epochs. Books break the shackles of time. A book is proof that humans are capable of working magic.*"

~Carl Sagan

20.

ALLOW ANGELS TO INSPIRE YOUR WRITING

I love the word creativity. Have you ever wondered where creative types find their ideas to paint, compose or write? Many artists know their best work comes "through" them rather than "from" them. Today, I'll call this muse an Angel, yet I've used and heard other names: God, Spirit, Guides, Higher Self, Automatic Writing, Inner Voice, to mention a few. John O'Donohue speaks of "those in the unseen world." There are books devoted to this topic, and yet, today I will share some of my own Angel assistance experiences, and maybe there will be an idea or two for you to use.

IN THE BEGINNING About 20 years ago, in the early hours between sleep and awake, I heard (with my ears), "Release the Material." That woke me up! I scrambled to find a pen and paper to record the message so I wouldn't forget it. *What the heck did it mean?* The next day I had a similar experience: another audible phrase. That's when I got serious, and put the two messages on a list. The next morning, I anxiously awaited the third message. But nothing came.

So I decided to relax my mind—and that day a phrase came to me from somewhere in my head. I was a little disappointed about not being able to "hear" the words (which was a very cool experience)—yet each day for the next 180 days or so, I sat down to receive. Some message was always given to me. Each was short and sweet, but comforting just the same.

ALLOWING Over the years, I came to realize that the more I cleared my mind, the more I received. Much has been written about meditation, and rightly so. By sweeping the random thoughts out of your mind, you have space to let something new come in. My advice is to experiment with various methods (sit, walk, read, dance, listen to music, or place yourself near water) to find out what works for you.

TRUST It's not really necessary to know that your inspiration comes from an Angel, your Higher Self, or a Spirit Guide. Simply consider these helpful messages without needing to know their exact source. The source of truth is within you, and so you can trust the "feel" of the message when it's been activated; it feels right to you, and it embodies love. In one chapter of my first book, *Rock Solid Confidence,* I found myself writing, "It's just like making a pizza…" As soon as I saw the words I'd written on the page, I stopped—judging it as an odd thing to say, wondering if it was a mistake—but soon, the rest came to me and it turned out to be a great analogy.

CLARITY A few years ago, I was working on a journal of messages composed of short sentences. Sometimes the messages made sense, but other times, I needed to make a request: *Give it to me in a different way—no one will be able to understand this.* And guess what? A new thought appeared in my mind and it was clearer. No matter where we look for inspiration, the author (you) is responsible to the reader (not the Angel), and so it is appropriate to be assertive.

ORDER We live in a world of order, but the Angels do not. I found this true when I was working on a set of

Goddess cards that included a three part description on the back. Sentences were given to me, but soon I realized that some sentences fit better in another section. It's perfectly fine to rearrange the message so that it can be readily understood by the reader. Many people feel that this type of writing is sacred, and they hesitate to change it or rearrange it, but go ahead. You're in charge.

AUTHOR   Being open to inspiration makes the writing process less lonely, however, be the leader. You are the one who needs to sit down in front of the computer to write, even when you don't "feel" like it, or Angels don't seem to be around to inspire you. During the final writing of my first book, I closed myself off in my office, looping a Yanni CD, with a lit candle, and incense—each day. I believe that when the author is ready to do the work, the Angels drop in to inspire and not the other way around. On the other hand, sometimes you'll be watching a movie, or talking to a friend when—POW—something is said that you *know* is a new bit meant to be included in your current project.

STRENGTHEN   Great books are like apple cider in that they are tastier with a rich blend of sources. Research additional information for your topic. (And don't put it past your Angels to point you to great keywords.) This strengthens your writing, so blend your inspiration with other sources that provide facts, statistics and stories.

GRATEFUL OWNERSHIP   Because you've allowed Angelic assistance, you may not feel worthy to take the credit for your writing. Yet you were the one who received the messages. You made 1,000 decisions, gave order to the topics, spent long hours and money to bring your writing into the world. Be grateful and give credit to your Angels, yet own your work. Be a proud author.

Your Conversation Questions:

Victoria Vaske is a master of marketing. She also studies astrology and raises her daughter to love herself. Spirit comes to her like a slow Sunday drive with the windows open. Hosting women's retreats is certainly in her future. These are Victoria's suggested discussion questions:

1. How do you feel Spirit (or Angels or God) talks to you? When do you feel that Spirit? Example: In the shower, while running.

2. What is your relationship with Trust? In other words, if Trust were a person sitting next to you in your car, how would you describe that relationship?

3. How do you make requests during your dialog with Angels (or Spirit)? What do you say? What do you ask for?

4. If you decide to strengthen your communication with the Divine, what sources would you use? Examples: meditation, yoga, time alone, sacred books.

5. Summarize ways that you have used to successfully focus your mind so you are ready to communicate with Spirit.

6. How does communicating with Spirit/Angels benefit your life?

21.

WRITING YOUR STORY: UNEXPECTED

BENEFITS

Great movies exaggerate life to make it easy for us to see our own patterns. *Jumanji: Welcome to the Jungle*, is no exception! If you remember, this action packed movie is about a group of young people, literally, thrown into a jungle game. In order to win, the players learn to work together. Each level of the game represents a frightening challenge in the quest to get home. Hair-raising, yet, if the main characters face no danger, there's no story.

I'd like to see it again so I can hear the dialog, get the characters straight in my mind, and catch more of the humor. Do you see the similarities between watching movies twice and writing about the adventures of your own life?

Think about it. Your life is also like a game with a gauntlet of problems. Since the future is unknown, you are not sure how things will work out, and you might cover your eyes, missing most of what's going on. Writing your story is re-living your life; like seeing a movie twice. The good news is, it's more fun because, win or lose, you are the survivor of your adventure.

Movies and life adventures can be divided into a clock with four sections, starting at the top of the hour:
1. we meet the character in a setting
2. a problem threatens the character, blocking the goal.
3. after a few mis-steps or failures, the problem gets solved
4. a resolution completes the story.

I'm learning a lot through presenting my story workshops, where participants metaphorically dive into their lives to search for their best stories. Before the first workshop, I did all the exercises myself to test them. I felt that if it worked for me, it would be beneficial for others.

While I was happy with the structure of the workshop, what surprised me was the joy I felt retelling my adventures—even small ones. Like watching a great movie twice, I got to enjoy the details, see how the relationships fit together, discovered the humor and note the lessons learned this second time around.

Untold stories are lost forever, so I encourage you to become your own scriptwriter. Partner with your trusty writing buddy, your computer. Dive in to find your story. Write as if you are sharing a grand adventure, because you are. You are the star of your own blockbuster, so shine into your happily ever after!

Your Conversation Questions:

Mary Whalen breathes generosity, curiosity and kindness. She is passionately Catholic. She has authored numerous articles and captured extraordinary photographs for local and national publications. Her joyful call to the vocation of motherhood has been realized in her amazing children and grandchildren. Here are Mary's suggested discussion questions:

1. Many of us watch famous old movies over and over again. When you see a famous movie—*The Wizard of Oz*, for example—how can seeing it as a child, a teen and an adult change your view of this movie?

2. How might your perspective change when viewing your own adventures through the eyes of a child, a teen and an adult? Has there been growth?

3. How might you change your view of your life if you viewed it as an "adventure"?

4. Can remembering some of the stories of your past add validity to your life's journey? Give an example from your life.

5. Do you agree or disagree with this statement: By examining someone else's life, you can discover the events that have made them who they are today. Explain.

6. How can laughter increase your connectedness to others?

22.

WHAT'S YOUR BEST SHOE STORY?

I love to hear shoe stories. My favorite workshop question is about shoes because everyone—EVERYONE—has at least one good shoe story to tell that makes them laugh, shake their head, and remember a moment that's been tucked away in the past. Our shoes are more than fashion statements. They take us *"...where we want to go and how we want to go,"* to re-purpose a John O'Donohue quote.

I spent a few hours one day focused on my own life, and I came up with four shoe stories for each of the three chapters of my life. **Just for fun, try it**. Write down a description of any specific shoes you remember wearing—just three or four words will capture and name your memory. Next, list them in chronological order. Then reflect on what ELSE the memory is about. Let me give you a quick example:

When I was about 20, I drove to Decorah with Diane, who lived near our farm. We were from the small town of Harmony, so Decorah represented a shopping mecca for us. We spent the day browsing through all the stores hunting for bargains.

We got excited when we saw the shoe store. In those days, shoes came in basic colors and styles, but the minute we stepped into the store, a silver pair of sandals, adorned with a row of four sparkly rhinestones on a chunky heel took us by surprise. We looked at each other and knew that wearing them would make us feel like queens.

Just then, the clerk burst our bubble by "indicating" that those shoes were far too expensive for either of us to buy. *How dare she think that!* Lucky for us, we both wore the same size, and long story short, we pooled our money and bought one pair of shoes to share. For the next few years, we took turns being flashy.

Stories are etched into our memories and once we remember the shoes, a wake follows. Memories reveal the type of journey we've been living—in other words, the shoes might not even be the main point of the shoe story.

Even though the subject of the story is *shoes*, it's really a story about *other elements of life.* Like other stories, shoe stories can be added to the many stories we tell each day, or used for a job interview example, to make a point in a speech or share with friends. Besides being a shoe story, my particular story is also about:

- the close friendship I had with Diane
- ways to be resourceful
- looking to others for approval
- not wanting to be considered poor
- what it was like to be a teenage girl

When I examined all 12 of my shoe stories, I discovered patterns and themes: four included men, two were fashion centered, two mentioned popular fairy tales, two were journeys, and two involved girlfriends. Yes, the simplest memories are a microcosm of a life, just as a bucket of ocean water is a part of the ocean.

So for a fun trip down memory lane, think shoes!

Your Conversation Questions:

Energetic Peggy Robbins, past state president (PSP) for California Chapter of P.E.O., continues to serves other Arizona chapters today. She was an award-winning Mary Kay representative, and excels at any work she takes on. Family and friends are her heartfelt gifts. These are Peggy's suggested discussion questions:

1. Which words do you associate with shoes? For example: Sensible, flirty, practical.

2. If you first became aware of fashion as a girl, how might the shoes your parents bought for you differ from those *you* wanted to wear?

3. There's something special about red shoes. Do you have a red shoe story? Besides the details of the shoes, what else is this story about?

4. Have you ever felt guilty for purchasing a pair of shoes? Where did that feeling come from?

5. What do your shoe choices say about your personality?

6. Besides the *Wizard of OZ*, which movie comes to mind that mentions or features shoes?

7. Peggy keeps a pair of her mother's boots. She cherishes them and will keep them forever. Have you kept a pair of shoes or an item of clothing from a loved one?

INVITATION

It is my hope that through reading and reflecting on some of the ideas of this book, you have gained a deeper appreciation of yourself and your journey. Perhaps you now regard yourself as a well seasoned person!

This is your invitation to join the Whalen Voices community. Here are a few suggestions:

1. If you want to know what's new with Whalen Voices, subscribe to our **monthly news** at: www.whalenvoices.com

2. Our most popular workshop is about writing your story. It features an ocean theme, where we dive for various stories from your past. If you're wondering how you could benefit from this experience, here are a few reasons you will find it helpful.

- Jump-start writing the story of your life
- Understand the origins of your values
- Uncover stories to use for job interviews
- Understand your "Why"
- Leave your legacy

3. If you want to start writing a book and need a quick way to begin, ask us about the VIP **Quick Start Private Book Coaching.** We'll take you from ideas to chapter titles in a few hours. Other workshops and private writing options are available on our website: www.whalenvoices.com

GRATEFUL

Just thinking about those who have supported the publication of this book makes my soul smile.

Quotes and inspiration came from: Janice Baiden, Brené Brown, Thom Browne, Wayne Dyer, Diane Ryan Guttormson, Natalie Goldberg, Carl Koch, Robert Lowe, Sheena Lyengar, Ross McCollum, Francois Mauriac, the late Ralph Hillman, Ph.D., Tony Robbins, Mike Roelofs, Scott Roelofs, Eric Whalen, JK Rowling, Betty Hahn, Ellis Vidler, LaRae Worden, my P.E.O. sister in Chapter Eternal—Anna Marie Peterson and so many others not named. Thank you all.

I'm grateful to the brilliant designer and friend, Diego Paredes, who worked with me to create this cover and "Chili Millie," who is making her debut into the world. Also, to Carol Waltz for backing me up with technical assistance for this project and many other projects. You're the best!

Huge thanks goes to those who shared their time with me to read and collaborate on questions for each chapter. You added the SPICE to this conversation! Thanks: Ruth Vaske, Patricia Tomlin, Amber Roelofs, Linda Garza Kalaf, Jamise Liddell, Ph.D., Dr. Len Whalen, Ralph Whalen, John Whalen, Sharon Foster, Ph.D., Laura Thomas, Ellen Whalen, Betty Johnson, Glenda Myers, Karen Needham, Sherry Munther, Karen Bahti, Julie Crooks, Adrienne McGill, Deb Frese, Nicole Kroebusch, Jerri Thomas, Darlene Schlicht, Victoria Vaske, Mary Whalen, and Peggy Robbins.

I'm grateful to other authors who wrote the following books to inspire me:

- *Anam Cara: A book of Celtic Wisdom*, John O'Donohue

- *Blue Mind: Mental Health Benefits of Being Near Water,* Wallace J. Nichols
- *Man's Search for Meaning* Victor E. Frankl
- *Powers of Two: Finding the Essence of Innovation in Creative Pairs,* Joshua Wolf Shenk
- *Rock Solid Confidence: Presenting Yourself with Assurance, Poise and Power; You are the Perfect Age,* Jan Whalen
- I also drew upon Ruth Chang's message in her TED Talk, "How to Make Hard Choices"

In so many ways, I observed and assimilated lessons from my Lean-In Group, the Whalen Family, my Board of Directors, and of course, my Spiritual Writing Team. Thank you for being there for me.

"No love, no friendship, can cross the path of our destiny without leaving some mark on it forever."

~Francois Mauriac

ABOUT THE AUTHOR

Jan M. Whalen lives in the Phoenix area with her husband Ross and enjoys being close to grandchildren. A native of Harmony, Minnesota and long time resident of Iowa, she brings a Midwest flavor to all she does.

Jan is a member of P.E.O. (Philanthropic Educational Organization) with terms as president for two different chapters; and recently served on the membership committee for the Arizona State Chapter. She has a Master of Arts degree in Servant Leadership, a black belt in Taekwondo, and a diverse work history in education, public relations, sales, and training.

Jan is an award winning author, keynote speaker, workshop leader, writing mentor and book creation coach. Her mission is to empower women through their own life stories.

Her book *You are the Perfect Age: Celebrate Your Life* has been so successful, she created a line of greeting cards called The Perfect Age® for you to send uplifting messages to the women in your circle of friends and family.

With all sincerity, Jan says, "I'd like to change the conversations we have with each other about our age. We are SEASONED with time, so let's celebrate our Perfect Age!"

Jan's website: www.whalenvoices.com
Call her at 623.466.5067
email: jan@whalenvoices.com

NOTES:

NOTES:

NOTES: